THE PALMER COX
BROWNIE PRIMER

ARRANGED FROM PALMER COX'S
BROWNIE BOOKS

TEXT BY MARY C. JUDD
PICTURES BY PALMER COX
GRADING AND EDITING
BY MONTROSE J. MOSES

PUBLISHED BY THE CENTURY CO.
NEW YORK . . . . ·1921

EDUCATION DEPT.

PREFACE

It is a mistaken idea that children learn to read only through bare, spiritless statement of fact. At no other period is imagination so naïvely active, and to the imaginative faculty the Brownies appeal.

The editors have arranged the text so as to repeat words constantly; they have likewise placed the subject matter in its proper season, beginning with the early Fall, when school opens. While definite lessons have been indicated on every page, it is to be hoped that the pictures in themselves will suggest to the teacher additional topics for talks and blackboard sentences, and at the same time furnish the interest and incentive to induce the child to learn to read the text. The Appendix contains directions for the use of the vocabulary and of those pages on which the play element is distinctly emphasized.

To understand the characteristics of the Brownies is the essential requisite for the understanding of this little Primer. The genial, hearty, and helpful spirit with which the little men are supposed always to go through their tricks, is largely the cause of the success they have had. May they find equal favor in the school room, while the children are learning to read.

PALMER COX.

CONTENTS

8   **Contents**

THE PALMER COX
BROWNIE PRIMER

THE PALMER COX BROWNIE PRIMER

Oh, see the flag.

Up with the flag.

Up with the flag on high.

Do you see the flag?

Hurrah for the flag!

Hurrah for the flag on high!

There is the red.

There is the white.

There is the blue.

The red, white, and blue.

One little Brownie.

One 1

Two little Brownies.

Two 2

Three little Brownie men.

Three 3

One   Two   Three

1   2   3

Four little Brownies.
Four 4

Five little Brownies.
Five 5

Six little Brownie men.
Six 6

Four	Five	Six
4	5	6

Seven little Brownies.
Seven 7

Eight little Brownies.
Eight 8

Nine little Brownies.
Nine 9

Ten little Brownie men.

The wise Brownie said: "Go to school."
"Yes, yes, we will go to school," said the little merry men.

'You must study."

"Yes, yes, we will study," said the little merry men.

"Oh, see, there is the school-house."

"Hurrah! let us go to school," said the little merry men.

"Run, run to the school-house."

"Study, study," said the wise Brownie.

Nine o'clock is school time.

Go to school, Brownies.

Here are your books and pads and pencils.

One Brownie tried to spell.

"B-r-o-w-n-i-e," he said.

And one Brownie tried to read.

And all the Brownies sang a song.

They sang, "Hurrah for the red, white, and blue."

But when daytime came, the Brownies ran away.

Why did the Brownies run away?

THE nights are long.
The nights are cold.
The apples are red.
The apples are ripe.
"Come," cried the Brownies, "come and let us go to the apple tree."
Look, how the apples fall on the ground.
Run, run, let us pick them up.
Hurry, hurry, for the nights are cold.
And the frost will come soon.
Here is a basket.
Put the apples in the basket.
Oh, what fun to pick the apples from the ground.
Take care, take care, little Brownies, don't fall.
The Brownie is in the tree.
Will he fall?
Tell us what you see, little Brownie.
"I see birds," he said.

See the cotton! How white it is.
The Brownies pick the cotton.
They put the cotton into the baskets.
Cotton grows like a flower.
Each flower is a soft white ball.
See the Brownie under the cotton.
Will it hurt the Brownie?
No, for cotton is very soft.
Hurry Brownies, it is nearly day.

Look, the Brownies are in the wheat
field.

The farmer must cut his wheat.

The little men will help the farmer.

What will they do with the wheat?

They will cut it and pile it up.

What is wheat, little Brownies?

"It is grain," said the little merry men.

In the morning, the farmer will say:
"Thank you, Brownies, for your help."

GUESS

(Adapted from St. Nicholas.)

He stands up straight against the wall—
The smallest Brownie of them all—
"Guess what I have behind me here?"
And then he laughs—this Brownie queer.

"A doll?"
"No."
"A ball?"
"No."
"A cat?"
"No."
"A hat?"
"No."
"Well, I'll confess
"I can't guess."

With outstretched arms, this Brownie
   stands
And says: "I only had my hands!"

THE MERRY LITTLE MEN

REVIEW

Hurrah! the red, white and blue!
Ten little Brownie men.
Go to school, you merry little men.
Look, how the apples fall on the ground.

WORD LIST

[Use these words in new sentences.]

little	flag
nearly	daytime
farmer	hurry
cotton	field
morning	flower
apple	basket
nine	o'clock

We went one night to
have our pictures taken.
Oh, what fun we had!
You will find more pictures of us in
this book.

The man said: "Smile!"

Find the
Soldier   Sailor
Chinaman   Indian

Up, up, up!
Over, over, and over!
One, two, three, up and over the
Brownies go!
See the elephant.
The elephant will not hurt the
Brownies.
Up, up, and over his back the merry
little Brownies go.
Up and over and down they go.
How very big the elephant is.
How very small the Brownies are.
They can jump over the elephant.
They can walk a rope.
They can have fun.

The elephant now goes round;
The band begins to play.
The Brownies in the circus ring
Had better keep away.

The apples are ripe.
    Where is the farmer?
And the pumpkin is ripe.
And the corn is not cut.
    Where is the farmer?
The farmer is sick; the farmer is sad.
Here come the Brownies to help him

Run, Brownie, run with
the foot-ball.

"Catch him,
catch him," cry
the little merry
men.

See the soldier with the ball.

"Hurrah, I have him by the legs," says
a Brownie.

Will he fall?

Yes, and another Brownie will get the
foot-ball.

Run, run, run with the foot-ball.

"Hurrah," cry the Brownies, "we have
won the game."

"Rah, rah, rah!"

"I am glad we won
the game. I am tired,"
said a Brownie.

So he sat down to rest
on the foot-ball.

Here a swing and there a swing.
Here a ring and there a ring.
How strong the Brownies are!
How happy the Brownies are!
Up and over they go!
Up the ladders and over the bars they go.
They will not fall.
Swing, Brownies, swing!   You happy
little men, you merry little men!
This is the way to get strong.

What shall the farmer have for his Thanksgiving dinner?

Turkey, turkey, turkey.

These turkeys belong to the farmer.

Let us take them to the house for the farmer. Then we will go home. We will have our Thanksgiving dinner.

When I am big, I mean to buy
A dozen platters of pumpkin pie,
A barrel of nuts, to have them handy,
And fifty pounds of sugar candy.

MARY MAPES DODGE.

One Brownie saws wood this way; another Brownie saws wood that way.

Take care, Brownies, the wood will fall, and then you will fall.

Here comes a Brownie with another log of wood.

Will you saw this log also, Brownies?

Whose wood is this, Brownies?   Is it the farmer's wood?

Is he in the house asleep?

Oh, merry little Brownies, how happy you must be to help.

REVIEW

Do you like the pictures of the Brownies in this book?

The Brownies can jump over the back of the elephant.

The apples are ripe; the pumpkin is ripe. Where is the farmer?

What shall the farmer have for his Thanksgiving dinner?

Did you see the Brownies go up the ladders and over the bars?

Run, Brownie, run with the foot-ball.

Where are the Brownies who saw wood?

WORD LIST

[Use these words in new sentences.]

ripe	another	asleep
catch	foot-ball	dinner
strong	soldier	turkey
happy	pumpkin	pictures
over	elephant	belong

WHAT DOES BROWNIE WANT?

(Adapted from St. Nicholas.)

DEAR SANTA CLAUS:

I don't want a thing that
girls would like;
I don't want a velocipede,
but a bike;
I don't want anything
to wear;
I don't want an apple
or a pear;
I don't want a ship
that won't sail;
I don't want a goody-goody tale.

BROWNIE.

Watching for Santa Claus

P. S.—I was just about not to say,
I don't want you to forget me Christmas Day.

The Brownies went into a toy-shop

They opened a box. Out jumped a queer man. His cap came off.

The Brownies found a toy rabbit.

Near the rabbit was a box of dolls.

Then the Brownies jumped on a hobby-horse.

What fun they had in the toy-shop with all the toys.

What a tall fence!

This is such a good peep-hole in the fence.

Did you ever look through a peep-hole?

What do you see, Brownie?

Three Brownies are looking over the fence. It is night. The sky is dark.

But the moon shines.

We can see the fence and the Brownies.

What do you see, Brownie Boys?

Are you looking at the moon?

Are you looking to see if it is time to run away?

Are you looking for the sun?

AT MORNING LIGHT.
WE TAKE OUR FLIGHT.

REVIEW.

What did the Brownies find in the toy-shop?

What did they do with the hobby-horse?

Did Brownie want a velocipede?

What do you think Santa Claus gave Brownie on Christmas Day?

What did Brownie see through the peep-hole? Did he see the moon?

Find the two Brownies on the log of wood.

DAYS OF THE WEEK

Sunday

Monday	Thursday
Tuesday	Friday
Wednesday	Saturday

Seven days make one week.

One, two, three, look out for the snowball!

Oh, a ball hit his crown.

Who hit you, Brownie, do you know?

Come and play with the other Brownies.

See the sticks of wood these Brownies have.

No, they are not sticks of wood. They are sticks of ice.

They are icicles from the trees.

Who is Jack Frost?

Ice and snow come in the winter time.

Here is a picture in the snow. Jack Frost did not make it. I know who made it. Do you?

Jingle, bells; jingle, bells;
Jingle all the way!
Oh! what fun it is to ride
With the Brownies in a sleigh!

"Hear the silver bells,
How they tinkle, tinkle, tinkle,
In the cold, cold air of night!
Oh! the swinging and the ringing
Of the bells, bells, bells."

We must find a Christmas tree.

Come, let us go to the woods, little Brownies.

We will cut down the Christmas tree.

Tramp, tramp, tramp!   How soft the snow is.

Hurry, there is a Christmas tree in the woods.

And I see a tall tree next to it.

Yes, we will cut down that tree also, and use it for a flag-pole.

How beautiful the flag will look waving on high.

Hurrah for the flag on high!

When the Brownies came to the woods, they cut down the Christmas tree. Then they climbed to the top of the other tree and cut off the branches.

"I can see far over the tops of the trees," called the Brownie who was up in the tree.

"Come, all of you," said the Brownie with the axe, "we must cut this tree down. Hurry, for to-morrow is Christmas."

Hurrah for Christmas!" said the Brownies.

Hurrah! Clear the way!
Here we come down the hill!
Hold fast, Brownies, hold fast.
Look, there is a Brownie up in the air.
Head over heels, up and over he goes.
Ha, ha! Some Brownies fell in the soft snow.
How smooth the snow is on the hill.
Down the hill we go; how very fast we go.

Clear the way.
Hurrah, hurrah!

REVIEW

When do ice and snow come?

Are icicles sticks of ice?

Did the Brownies make the picture in the snow?

Tinkle, tinkle, tinkle, hear the ringing of the bells.

Where did the Brownies find the Christmas tree?

Did the Brownies bring the flagpole home in the sleigh?

What fun the smooth snow is on the hill!

WORD LIST

[Use these words in new sentences.

Jack	snowball	Christmas
Frost	icicles	waving
sleigh	picture	beautiful
tramp	jingle	branches
ringing	swinging	to-morrow

[By taking the lines separately and together, and by making combinations of the different lines, the teacher will be able to give elementary drills in addition and subtraction.]

Oh, what a big ball of snow.

Look out, there is a Brownie under the ball of snow.

Let us make a snow man.

Here is snow for his arms and legs.

Here are four icicles for his hair.

And here is one icicle for his finger.

Look at the snow man the Brownies made.   He is very big.

"We are small," said the Brownies.

When daylight came, the Brownies ran away.

Cold January
brings the snow.

JANUARY

nd winds in February blow.

FEBRUARY

In March the winter turns
to go.

MARCH

In April seeds begin to grow.

APRIL

Bright May brings sunshine, fruit, and
   flowers;
And s i n g i n g
birds and happy
    hours.

MAY

In June the nights are bright and
   clear,
      And roses fill the land with
      cheer.

JUNE

Oh, sunny-faced is hot
July,
The time when all the flags do
fly.

JULY

      In August people
      go away,
   That is the time
    for holiday.

AUGUST

September, with its falling leaves,
And golden grain
piled up in sheaves.

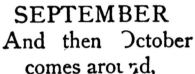

SEPTEMBER

And then October
comes around,
With apples red upon
the ground.

OCTOBER

November, dear to
people gay,
Because it brings
Thanksgiving
Day.

NOVEMBER

And cold December, Christmas
brings,
With happiness and toys and
things!

DECEMBER

THE MONTHS

January	July
February	August
March	September
April	October
May	November
June	December

Twelve months make a year.

January—Snow   July—Sun
February—Ice   August—Holiday
March—Winds   September—Leaves
April—Seeds   October—Apples
May—Flowers   November—Turkey
June—Roses   December—Toys

First one Brownie went on the ice,
then another, and another, and another.

By and by all the Brownies were on
the ice with their skates.

One little Brownie fell on his back.
Did he cry? No, no,—up and away he
went!

Some Brownies skated this way and
some skated that way.

They skated everywhere on the ice.

Who cut the large *B* on the ice?

Once there was a little
Brownie. He knew how
to skate on the ice.

One winter night he
put his skates on. He
made the first letter of his name
on the ice.

There was another Brownie,
who did not know how to skate.
His feet went up in the air,
and he fell down on the ice.

Then there was
still another Brownie. He
could skate on roller skates.
So the Chinaman got on his
back. And there were two little
Brownies who came together,
bang! And
their feet went up in
the air. But they were
not hurt.

These little Brownies are in Japan.
Each Brownie has a Japanese parasol.
How many Japanese parasols can you
see?　Nine, ten,—which is right?
Do they have Brownies in Japan?
Have you ever been far from home?
One little Brownie is in the dark.
What has he in each hand?
He has a Japanese lantern.
Have you seen a Japanese lantern?

The Child:

Tell me truly, Brownie man,
  Which way does the wind blow?
Tell me truly, if you can,
  Do you know?

The Brownie:

North or south or east or west,
Which wind do you like best?
Watch the weather-vane and see
Which wind this wind may be.
Watch the arrow turn; it knows
Which way the wind blows.

REVIEW

Did the Brownies skate on the ice?

What letter did the Brownie cut on the ice?

Did the Brownie fall on the ice?

Was the Brownie hurt when he fell down on the ice?

Have you ever seen roller skates? The little Brownie with the Chinaman on his back had on roller skates.

When the Brownies were in Japan, they had Japanese parasols.

One Brownie had a Japanese lantern.

Have you ever seen a Japanese para-sol or a Japanese lantern?

WORD LIST

[Use these words in new sentences.]

North	weather-vane	South
East	arrow	West
skate	Chinaman	parasol
home	wind	lantern

Did you ever see the great clouds in the sky? Did you ever wish to ride upon the clouds as they sailed away?

That would be as fine as sailing in a boat. But what if you should fall? You would need to be a Brownie then, or you would be hurt.

How did the Brownies get up there?

I do not know. You must catch a Brownie some day and ask him.

Sailing away, sailing away, and the wind is blowing softly, softly.

How will they come down again? Maybe it will rain and they will ride down on the rain-drops, or on the snow. They are not afraid; they are safe.

Come, come, let us sing a song.

Shall we sing, "America"?

All right, hold your music before you.

Now, what is our country?

The United States is our country.

The Pilgrims came here, years ago, to find a home.

They came to this sweet land of liberty.

Now, let the band play, and—one, two, three—sing, Brownies; sing, "America."

"AMERICA"

My country, 't is of thee,
Sweet land of liberty,
   Of thee I sing;
Land where my fathers died,

Land of the pilgrim's
   pride,
From every mountain side
   Let freedom ring.

LOOK AT THE CLOCK.

What time do you get up in the morning?

What time do you go to bed at night?

What time do you go to school?

What time do you come home from school?

What time do you think the Brownies run away?

1-2-3-4-5-6-7-8-9-10-11-12.

REVIEW

What did the Brownies sing?

Do you know how to sing the song, "America"?

Would you like to hear the Brownies sing "America"?

Will the clock tell you when the Brownies run away?

Would you like to ride upon the clouds?

WORD LIST

[Use these words in new sentences.]

United States

music   Pilgrims

country   liberty

clock

clouds

SOME BROWNIE *DONT'S*

Don't spill  over your book.

Don't break the

Don't let a 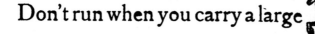 sting you

Don't run when you carry a large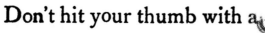

Don't hit your thumb with a

The Brownies can see in the dark.
But they cannot see in a fog.
The fog was thick one night.
The Brownies said: "We cannot see."
But each Brownie carried a lantern.
It is dark when the moon does not shine.
It is darker when the stars are not out.
It is darkest when there is fog.
Fog looks like smoke.
It hides the moon and the stars

A windmill, a windmill! The Brownies have found a windmill!

See the big wheel. How the wind turns it!

Hold on, Brownies, or you will fall.

See the five Brownies peeping through the roof.

See the Brownies here and there and everywhere.

Round and round go the arms of the wheel.

No one can use the mill; it is such an old mill.

The miller has a new mill for his wheat.

Where is the miller? The miller is in bed and asleep.

The wind turns the wheel; the wheel helps to grind the grain.

"Stop turning the wheel, O wind, for it is nearly day, and we must go," the Brownies cry.

Where is the Chinaman?
He wears a pig-tail.
See the policeman?
He has a club in his hand.
Ye-ho! see the sailor.
What a long oar he holds.
Find the Brownie with the flag.
Why does he stand by the track?
Toot, toot, toot! This little
Brownie man blows a horn.
And see the little Brownie
with his bow and
arrow.
Six Brownies are
on this page.

Find the Brownie and
the big fan.
Find the telephones.
How many do
you see?
And how
many Brownies at each
telephone?
Hello, is that you,

Brownie?
Yes, this is
Brownie. How
are you?

I am very well, thank you.
How are you.
I am very well, too. Good-bye.
Where is the Brow-
nie with the flute?
Do you remember
one Brownie blew a
horn? Where is he?

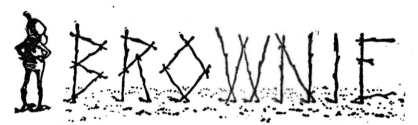

There is a Brownie with a spade.

It is April.   Make your garden in April, Brownies.

Here are two little Brownies with seed.

The Indian has seed, and another little Brownie has a rake.

Dig and rake, little Brownies.   Plant seed in April.

By and by the flowers will come.

See the sticks in the ground.

The vines will grow on the sticks.

Where do robins sleep at night?
The little robins sleep in their nests.
Where do squirrels sleep at night?
The squirrels sleep in holes in the trees.
Where do the Brownies sleep?
Who ever saw a Brownie asleep?
Maybe the Brownies do not go to sleep.

The birds have been singing to-day,
  And saying: "The spring is near!
The sun is as warm as in May,
  And the deep blue sky is clear."

JOHN ADDINGTON.

REVIEW

Did the Brownie spill ink over his books?

Did the Brownie break the glass?

Did a bee sting the Brownie?

Did the Brownie run with the large book?

Did the Brownie hit his thumb with a hammer?

What did the Brownies do in the fog?

Do you think the Brownies had fun at the mill, while the miller was in bed and asleep?

When will the flowers come?

WORD LIST
[Use these words in new sentences.]

nests	robins	telephone
spade	squirrels	flute
rake	policeman	miller
vines	sailor	ground

Do you remember the Brownies with the Japanese parasols?

And the little Brownie in the dark, with two Japanese lanterns?

Well, this is the way the Brownies used to ride in far-away Japan.

There are three Brownies at one end and two at the other end.

What a very queer way to take a ride.

Run, Brownies, run! You must go fast, for you must see many things before day comes.

What fun it is to travel!

One evening, just as the sun was going down, Brownie Boy rode away on his bicycle. Down the hill he went. "What fun!" he said.

But soon he had to ride through the sand, and that was not much fun.
Push, push, push.

Then he saw a long hill. Up went his legs, and away the bicycle rolled.

Brownie Boy did not even hold on to the handle-bars.

He let the bicycle go faster and faster down the hill.

Hurrah for the little Brownie!

And now, what do
you think! Brownie
Boy got on his bicy-
cle, just as you see
him in the picture.
Oh, what fun!

After a little while, he
did another trick, but his
wheel struck a stone and
over he went. Poor little
Brownie Boy!

'It 's time to go
home," he said, "for the
sun will be up soon."
So he rode and rode
and rode, until he came
to where the Brownies
hide in the day time.

Do you know where the Brownies
hide when they run away?

THE SEASONS

Spring
Summer
Autumn
Winter

REVIEW

Did the Brownie have fun when he went down hill on his bicycle?

How did he feel when he had to ride through the sand?

Was he a wise Brownie to let go the handle-bars?

Do you think the Brownie was hurt when his wheel struck the stone?

How did the Brownies ride in far-away Japan?

Was it a queer way for them to ride?

"Oh, let us go a-fishing,"
  Said the Brownie to his
    mate,
"You get the rods and
    basket
    While I run and get
    the bait.
Then we'll sit down by the river,
And we'll catch the fish that bite,
And we'll put them in the basket,
And be home before daylight."
So the Brownies went a-fishing,
  And they pulled the fellows out;
They looked at them but did not know
  A blue fish from a trout.
But any way the fun they had
  Was what the Brownies wished;
I wonder if 'twas fun for all
  The fish those Brownies fished.

SPRING SONG.

OH, the flowers that bloom in the
    Spring, tra, la—
And the little blue birds that sing, tra, la—
The daisy and rose,
And the green grass that grows,—
Oh, the little new birds on the wing, tra, la!

What do the Brownies say?

"Oh, I wish the winter would go,
    And I wish the summer would come.
Then the big brown farmer will hoe,
    And the little brown bee will hum."

H. O. KNOWLTON.

HILE Brownies stood
beneath the trees,
They heard the hum of
hidden bees.
They saw tne branches in the air;
They listened at the roots with care.

And then they tried to drive
the bees
From oui their hives within
the trees.
But oh, the bees spread out
their wings,
And hurt the Brownies with
their stings.

If you will let the bees alone—
The workers
and the lazy
drone—
They'll never think of
stinging you,
But honey they'll be bringing you.

REVIEW

Would you like to catch fish?

What would you do with the fish?

Would you put them in a basket?

Is it fun to fish?

What blooms in the Spring?

Do you wish the winter would go?

Do you wish the summer would come?

Will the farmer hoe the ground?

Would you hurt the bees?

What did the Brownies say about the bees?

Will you let the bees alone?

WORD LIST

[Use these words in new sentences.]

mate	river	wished
rods	basket	fished
bait	fellow	branches
blue	daisy	lazy
green	listened	honey

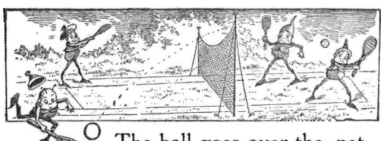

The ball goes over the net.
There goes another!

One Brownie has hit the ball with his racket.

Four rackets and four Brownies, but there are only two balls.

The Brownies are out on the lawn.

They are playing lawn-tennis.

Will the Brownie hit the ball with his racket?

Maybe he will, if he is quick.

Run, Brownie! try to hit the ball.

One Brownie has lost his hat.

He has no hair on his head; only two little butterfly horns are there.   How queer!

Do you like to play lawn-tennis?

Three merry Brownies on a donkey!
The Brownies do not hit the donkey.
The Brownies like to ride.
One Brownie says: "Get up, donkey!"
Another says: "Go on, donkey!"
And another says: "Good donkey!"
What are the others riding on?
It is a reindeer.   It has big horns.
It lives in the cold, cold north.

Blow your horns, Brownies.

Blow louder and louder. Who can hear such a little squeak?

Do you play in the Brownie band? Why can we never hear you in the night time?

Blow, blow, while the other Brownies dance.

Oh, this is such fun for the little merry men!

See the dancers lift their feet. One, two, three, and away they go.

Brownies, why will you not dance with us in the day time?

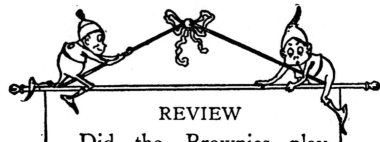

REVIEW

Did the Brownies play lawn-tennis?

How many Brownies and how many rackets were there?

Would you like to ride on a donkey or on a reindeer?

Did you know the Brownies could dance?

How many Brownies were in the Brownie band?

This is the way to
make a kite:
Get some paper
and get some
sticks;
Get some flour all
pure and white;

Pour in some water
and mix and
mix;

Strings for a tail;
then paste to-
gether,
And, ho! to the fields, for it"s kite
weather.

Take care, you will let the pail fall.
It is too large for Brownies to hold.
See how the water runs over the side.
Drink fast, horse, or the pail will fall.
Will you give the Brownies a ride?
Are you glad to drink the water?
Then you will be glad to give the little
Brownies a ride.
The Brownies came to give you water.
Drink fast, horse, drink fast.

See the horses in a row.
How fast they run!
No horse is ahead.
Do you think the black horse will soon
be ahead?
One Brownie has lost his hat.
Get up, black horse, get up!

Do you remember how to make a kite?

What do you do with the paper, the sticks, and the flour?

Does a kite have a tail?

Would you like to give a horse some water to drink?

Who won the race? Did the black horse win?

Hurrah for the black horse!

Run, run, run! Just see how many Brownies there are!

Can you find the Indian? the sailor?

Why do they run? It is almost day. Look at the sun.

What a long bridge; what a strong bridge this is across the river.

The river is wide; the river is deep.

See the Brownies go over this bridge across the river.

The bridge is made of wood. It is a strong bridge and a long bridge.

It is so long that the Brownies must run, for daytime is coming.

This is the way to carry a boat.

And this is the way to paddle a boat when it is in the water.

Do you know how to paddle?

And this is the way to bail a boat when it is full of water.

Do you know how to bail a boat?

The Brownies carried a boat to the water.

They got into the boat, and paddled through the water.

They saw the boat fill with water.

So they began to bail the boat.

One Brownie used a hat to bail with.

Then what do you think?

The Brownies fell into the water.

Learn to carry a boat to the water.

Learn to paddle through the water.

Learn to bail a boat when it is full of water.

But do not try to bail a boat with your hat.

Learn to swim.

E must learn to swim in the sea.

Do you remember when we were in the boat, and we fell into the water?

Tie a rope around Brownie Boy, and teach him how to swim.

Move your hands and feet, Brownie Boy, while you are in the water.

That is the way to swim.

When we know how to swim, we will have fun.

Yes, we will have fun in the water.

Hurrah!   Hurrah!

See, there is a Brownie who knows how to swim.   Watch his hands and feet.

He has a Brownie on his back.

Brownie, swim to the shore.

BROWNIE,
WHAT IS THE MATTER?

WHAT do you see in there?
Are you looking at yourself?
No, I am looking at little
drops of water. How very large they are!

Yes, the glass makes
the drops of water seem
larger than they are.

Oh, little Brownie, let
me look too.

Why, yes, how large the
little drops of water look!

See the other glass! What are you
doing with it, little Brownie?

I am looking at a frog.
Does the frog seem
larger when you look
at it through the glass?
Yes; have you ever
seen a glass like this?

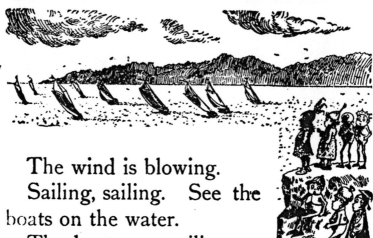

The wind is blowing.

Sailing, sailing.   See the boats on the water.

The boats are sailing on the sea.

The wind is blowing and the boats are sailing.

Which way does the wind blow?

How many boats do you see?

Nine boats: 1, 2, 3, 4, 5, 6, 7, 8, 9.

Sailing, sailing, through the water they go!

Hurrah, the boats are running a race! The wind is in the sails.

Ye-ho! which boat do you think is ahead, Brownies?

The Brownies are going to sea in a boat.

What will they take with them?

They have a large round box with a star in it.

What is it?

It is a compass.

It tells you where the North is.

Point North, point South, point East, point West.

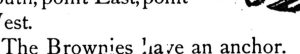

The Brownies have an anchor.

Now they are ready to go.

Sail away, Brownies, for the wind is blowing and the weather is fine.

Now, Brownies, stop the boat.

One, two, three, over goes the anchor into the water.

Hurrah!

Sand, sand, sand by the sea.
What fun we will have with our spades and pails.
Brownies, dig the sand by the sea.
Put the sand in your pails.
Oh, what fun it is by the sea!
Soon the sea will creep up on the sand, and then go back again.
Brownies, dig with your spades in the soft sand.
Hurry, it will be morning soon.

AT THE SEA-SIDE.

When I was down beside the sea
A wooden spade they gave to me
To dig the sandy shore.

My holes were empty like a cup.
In every hole the sea came up,
Till it could come no more.

ROBERT LOUIS STEVENSON

Look, Brow-
nie Boy, see
what I have on
my pad.
I have printed
July 4.

Let us find the other Brownies.

Then we will go with our fire crackers
and sky rockets to the field.

What a great noise the fire crackers
will make!

How pretty the sky rockets will be
with their ...

A sky rocket once scared a
Brownie.

It went with a big sound—
zwish—into the sky.

We must take care this
Fourth of July, must we not,
little Brownie Boy?

Hurry, hurry, we must find the other
Brownies and have fun with them.

Hurrah for the Fourth of July!
Hurrah for the flag!
Hurrah for the star spangled banner!
Come, let us sing with joy!

REVIEW

Why did the Brownies run across the long bridge and the strong bridge?

Do you know how to carry a boat to the water?

Did the Brownie try to bail the boat with his hat?

How did Brownie Boy learn to swim in the water?

Did the glass the Brownie had make the drops of water seem larger?

Have you ever seen sailboats run a race?

What will the Brownies do with the compass and the anchor?

Do you like the Fourth of July with its fire crackers and sky rockets?

What do you do in the sand when you go to the seashore?

Have you a spade and a pail?

Where do the Brownies live?

Why are the Brownies running away?
They were having fun, and they did
not see the sun peep over the hills.

The sun nearly caught them this time.
Who has ever seen a Brownie?

With a friendly wave of hand.
Now retires the Brownie band.

Dear children: Now the task is through,
But ere we part, a word with you—
Yes, you who traveled hand in hand
With me to watch the Brownie band,
May *you* prove always stanch and true
To teachers and to playmates too.
Be brave when trials fast descend,
And persevering to the end,
And, Brownie-like, you may be blessed—
They seldom fail who do their best.

Yours very truly,
Palmer Cox,

THE END

APPENDIX

VOCABULARY

A paragraph only is necessary regarding the play-element in this book; the drawing suggestion presented on page 17 should be followed by many exercises of a similar character, prepared by the teacher; the shadow pictures on page 23 should be used as bases for stories to be "imagined" by the pupils; and the counting lesson on page 45 might be studied in the form of a game.

Words found in this phonetic vocabulary are contained in those lessons intended to be taught to the pupils. There are some jingles which have been inserted as memory exercises, and words therein contained are not here included. Those verses occur on pages 22, 31, 34, 39, 55, 59, 60, 71, 77, 78, 79, 85, 89. Page 102 is to be read aloud and explained by the teacher.

PRONUNCIATION KEY TO THE PALMER COX BROWNIE PRIMER. BASED ON THE LATEST EDITION OF "THE CENTURY DICTIONARY."

a   as in fat, man, pang.
ā   as in fate, mane, dale.
ä   as in far, father, guard.
â   as in fall, talk.
à   as in ask, fast, ant.
ậ   as in fare.
e   as in met, pen, bless.
ē   as in mete, meet.
ê   as in her, fern.
i   as in pin, it.
ī   as in pine, fight, file.
o   as in not, on, frog.
ō   as in note, poke, floor.
ŏ   as in move, spoon.
ô   as in nor, song, off.
u   as in tub.
û   as in mute, acute.
ṷ   as in pull.

ü   German ü, French u.
oi as in oil, joint, boy.
ou as in pound, proud.

A single dot under a vowel in an unaccented syllable indicates its abbreviation and lightening, without absolute loss of its distinctive quality.

ạ   as in prelate, courage.
ẹ   as in ablegate, episcopal.
ọ   as in abrogate, eulogy.
ụ   as in singular, education.

A double dot under a vowel in an unaccented syllable indicates that, even in the mouths of the best speakers, its sound is variable to, and in ordinary utterance actually becomes, the short u-sound (of but, pun, etc.).

ạ   as in errant, republican.
ẹ   as in prudent, difference.

ị   as in charity, density.
ọ   as in valor, actor, idiot.
ᶳ   as in Persia, peninsula.
ḫ   as in the book.
ṵ   as in nature, feature.

A mark (~) under the consonants t, d, s, z indicates that they in like manner are variable to ch, j, sh, zh.

ṭ   as in nature, adventure.
ḍ   as in arduous, education.
ṣ   as in pressure.
ẓ   as in seizure.

th as in thin.
TH as in then.
D = TH.

' denotes a primary, " a secondary accent. Silent letters are italicized.

104

Page 11
with (wiᴛʜ)
hīgh
dŏ
you (yŏ)
hur-rah (hŏ-rä´)
fôr
there (ᴛʜär)
whīte (hwīt)
blue (blŏ)

Page 12
lit'tle
Brownie
(brou'ni)
two (tŏ)
thrēe

Page 13
fōur
fīve

Page 14
sev'en
eight (āt)
nīne

Page 15
wīse
said (sed)
school (skŏl)
wē
merry (mer'i)
study (stud'i)
tŏ

Page 16
o'clock (ǫ-klok´)

your (yŏr)
pencils
(pen'silz)
trīed
rēad
ållʔ
sŏng
they (ᴛʜā)
when (hwen)
away (ạ-wā´)
why (hwī)

Page 18
nights (nīts)
lŏng
rīpe
crīed
trēe
look (lŭk)
fållʔ
them (ᴛʜem)
hurry (hur'i)
frŏst
soon (sŏn)
bȧs'ket
what (hwot)
tāke
cãre
dŏn't
birds (bèrdz)

Page 20
cotton
(kot'n)
white (hwīt)
in'tŏ
grows (grōz)
līke

flower (flou'èr)
ēach
sôft
ballʔ
un'dèr
hurt (hèrt)
very (ver'i)
nearly (nèr'li)

Page 21
wheat (hwēt)
fīeld
fär'mèr
with (wiᴛʜ)
pīle
grāin
môr'ning
sāy
thank (thangk)
fôr

Page 25
night (nīt)
pictures
(pik'tūrz)
tȧk'en
find
mōre
of (ov)
this (ᴛʜis)
book (bŭk)
smīle
soldier (sōl'jèr)
sailor (sā'lǫr)
Chī'nȧ-man
In'di-ạn

Page 26
o'vèr

elephant
(el'ẹ-fạnt)
hurt (hèrt)
smallʔ
walʔk
rōpe

Page 27
goes (gōz)
bẹ-gins´
plāy
circus
(sèr'kus)
better (bet'èr)
kēep

Page 28
where (hwãr)

pump'kin
côrn

Page 29
foot (fŭt)
caʔch
says (sez)
another
ạ-nuᴛʜ'èr
gāme
tīred

Page 30
strông
happy (hap'i)
ladders
(lad'èrz)
bars (bärz)
wāy

Page 31
shall
Thanks-giv'ing
dinner
  (din'ẽr)
turkey (tẽr'ki)
these (ᴛнēz)
belong
  (bẹ-lŏng')
them (ᴛнem)
then (ᴛнen)
hōme

Page 32
saws (sâz)
wood (wŭd)
that (ᴛнat)
also (âl'sō)
whose (hŏz)
asleep
  (ạ-slēp')

Page 33
līke
who (hŏ)

Page 35
toy (toi)
opened (ō'pnd)
ŏ̞ff
rab'bit
nẽar
hobby-horse
  (hob'i-hôrs)

Page 36
tâll
fence (fens)
good (gŭd)
pēep
hōle
ev'ẽr
through (thrŏ)

looking
  (lŭk'ing)
därk
moon (mŏn)
shincs

Page 37
wĕck
Sun'dą̄y
Mon'day
  .(mun'dą̄)
Tuesday
  (tūz'dą̄)
Wednesday
  (wenz'dą̄)
Thursday
  (thẽrz'dą̄)
Fri'dą̄y
Saturday
  (sat'ẽr-dą̄)
māke
snōw

Page 38
knōw
other
  (uᴛн'ẽr)
these (ᴛнēz)
icicles
  (īs'i-kls)
win'tẽr
māde

Page 39
jingle
  (jing'gl)
rīde
sleigh (slā)

Page 40
Christmas
  (kris'mạs)
woods (wŭdz)
tâll

use (ūz)
pōle
beautiful
  (bū'ti-fŭl)
wă'ving

Page 41
when (hwen)
climbed (klīmd)
branches
  (brảnch'ẹz)
fär
called (kâld)
axe (aks)
tomorrow
  (tǒ-mor'ō)

Page 43
clear (klēr)
fàst
ãịr
head (hed)
heels (hēlz)
hă
some (sum)
smooth
  (smŏᴛн)

Page 46
arms (ärmz)
hair (hār)
finger
  (fing'gẽr)
smâll
light (līt)

Page 48
January
  (jan'ụ̄-ạ̄-ri)
February
  (feb'rǒ̞-ạ̄-ri)
blow (blō)
Märch
April (ā'prĭl)

sēeds
bẹ̄-gin'
grōw

Page 49
brĭght
Māy
sun'shīne
fruit (frŏt)
hours (ourz)
June (jön)
roses (rōz'ẹz)
chēer
sunny (sun'i)
faced (fāst)
July (ju-li')
August
  (â'gust)
pēo'ple
hol'i-dāy

Page 50
Sep-tem'bẽr
fâll'ing
leaves (lēvz)
gŏl'den
pīled
shēaves
October
  (ọk-tō'bẽr)
ạ-round'
Nọ̄-vem'bẽr
dēar
because
  (bẹ̄-ᴋâz')
December
  (dẹ̄-sem'bẽr)
hap'pi-nesս

Page 52
first (fẽrst)
skă'tẹd
ạverywhere
  (ev'ri-hwăr)

Page 53
once (wuns)
let′tėr
nâme
roller (rō′lėr)
together
(tŏ̱-geᴡ̱ᴇ′ėr)

Page 54
these (ᴡ̱ᴇ̆z)
Jap-a̱-nēse′
par′a̱-sol
many (men′i)
which (hwich)
rī̆ght
been (bĕn)
ēach
lan′tėrn

Page 57
grēat
sāi̱led
fine
sāi′ling
bōat
shoừld
nēed
woừld
âsk
blōw′ing
softly (sŏft′li)
māy′bė̱
rāin
a̱-frāi̱d′
sāfe

Page 58
America̱
(a̱-mer′i-ka̱)
music
(mū′zik)
bė̱-fōre′

country
(kun′tri)
ụ-nī′ted
stâtes
pil′grims
yĕars
a̱-gō′
swĕet
liberty
(lib′ėr-ti)

Page 61
shīnes
clock
dŏ′ing

Page 62
ė̱-lev′en
twelve
mŏr′ning
hōme

Page 64
brė̆ăk
carry (kar′i)
thumb

Page 65
cannot
(kan′ot)
thick
car′ried
dărk′ėr
dărk′ẹst
smōke
hīdes
stărs

Page 67
wind′mill
wheel (hwĕl)
pĕe′ping
roof (rŏf)

ōld
mill′ ėr
grīnd
turning
(tėr′ning)

Page 68
weărs
pig′tăil
ōar
toot (tŏt)
bōw
arrow (ar′ō)
page (păj)

Page 69
telephones
(tel′ė̱-fōnz)
heɭ-lō′
thank (thangk)
flute (flŏt)
rė̱-mem′bėr
blew (blö)

Page 70
spāde
găr′den
răke
vīnẹs

Page 71
squirrels
(skwur′elz)

Page 73
rīde
făr′a̱-wāy′
trav′el

Page 74
ēve′ning
bicycle
(bī′si-kl)

ŏ′ven
han′dle
fâs′tėr

Page 75
while (hwīl)
stōne
soon (sŏn)
rōde
un-til′

Page 76
summer
(sum′ėr)
autumn
(â′tum)

Page 78
bloom (blŏm)
daisy (dā′zi)
grēen
grăss

Page 81
rack′et
only (ōn′li)
lăwn
ten′nis
quick (kwik)
lŏst
butterfly
(but′ėr-flī)

Page 82
donkey
(dung′ki)
reindeer
(răn′dėr)
līvẹs

Page 83
loud′ėr
hėar

squeak
  (skwēk)
nev'ẽr
dance (dȧns)
dancer
  (dȧn'sẽr)

Page 86
pāil
too (tŏ)
sīde
drink (dringk)

Page 87
rŏw
ahead (a-hed')
black (blak)

Page 89
almost
  (âl'mōst)

bridge (brij)
across (a-krôs')
wide
dēep

Page 90
pad'dle
bȧil
full

Page 91
lẽarn

Page 92
sēa
tīe
rŏpe
a-round'
tēach
watch (woch)
shōre

Page 93
mat'tẽr
yourself
  (yŏr-self')
wȧ'tẽr
glȧss
sēem
larger
  (lȧrj'ẽr)

Page 94
run'ning

Page 95
compass
  (kum'pas)
anchor
  (ang'kor)
ready (red'i)
weather
  (wewH'ẽr)

Page 96
creep (krēp)
again (a-gen')

Page 98
print'ẹd
fire
crackers
  (krak'ẽrz)
rock'ets
noise (noiz)
pretty (prit'i)
scāred

Page 99
fōwrth

Page 101
caught (kȧt)

LaVergne, TN USA
18 November 2009
164529LV00005B/220/A